T0145304

SHARPOINT PUBLICATIONS

Guide for the Successful Trustee

…or for anyone trying to bring a little
organization into their financial life…

GUIDE FOR THE SUCCESSFUL TRUSTEE

Guide for the Successful Trustee

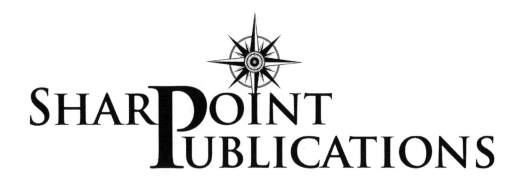

With Special Thanks To: Dean and Nancy Finley Couldn't Have Done It With Out You Two
Donna Finley – Thanks for the Perspective and the Patience
For Taking the Time to Teach – William R. Locklin and Forrest F. Wolfe
For Your Words of Encouragement – Bruce Athon and Kim Smith
For All Those Hours of Computer Time – N. Kent Demuth
For Help and Support - Bob Earhart and Kip Sturgeon
For the Early Days - Laurie Markovitch

ISBN: 978-1-4525-4681-0 (sc)

Library of Congress Control Number: 2012905864

Balboa Press books may be ordered through booksellers or by contacting:

Balboa Press
A Division of Hay House
1663 Liberty Drive
Bloomington, IN 47403
www.balboapress.com
1-(877) 407-4847

Printed in the United States of America

Balboa Press rev. date:4/12/2012

BALBOA
PRESS
A DIVISION OF HAY HOUSE

GUIDE FOR THE SUCCESSFUL TRUSTEE

Table of Contents

Overview

Section 1 -- Creation of Estate Plan – A well designed trust strategy is a powerful tax reduction and estate transfer tool. Section 1 of The Guide provides you with the documents needed to successfully transfer your assets to your new trust.

Section 2 - Transition of Estate Plan – The first event in the estate transfer process has occurred. Your spouse or one of your parents has passed away. What actions do you need to take and what paper work needs to be completed at this time?

Section 3 - Distribution of Estate Plan – You have been appointed executor/trustee; now what should you do? If trustees have followed this guide and kept it up to date, it should be a breeze. This section provides you with tools you need to complete the distribution.

Preface

When my uncle Bob informed me a few years ago that he had amended his living trust naming me as trustee, I was very flattered. My uncle was a shrewd investor and a sharp 'money man'. He knew his way around the tax code and rarely missed a trick when it came to his finances. No one knew the value of his estate. I guessed at the time that his net worth was well over $1,000,000. Being appointed to handle his estate was an expression of trust on his part that I was honored to receive.

Bob didn't have a favorite investment product. He owned a little of everything: CDs, mutual funds, life insurance, stocks, bonds, variable and fixed annuities, REITs. He fully funded his IRAs, 403(b)s and supplemental retirement plans. He used banks, credit unions, brokerage houses and discount traders.

He was well diversified, but his investments were an organizational nightmare. He was like many successful investors. He enjoyed the hunt. He liked doing the analysis work and tracking his choices and he was good at it. The problem was he kept most of this financial information in his head. When it came to a system for monitoring his holdings he had none, or at least none that has been found. He had 5 safe deposit boxes, a home safe and his freezer for storing documents. Nowhere could a list be found of what he owned or how he owned it.

When Living Trusts became popular in the 1980s he was one of the first to sign up. He could see the tax benefits to his heirs that a living trust provided. He had firsthand knowledge of the difficulties in administering an estate from his work on behalf of his parents' estate. He understood which assets had to be owned by the trust and which did not. Even though it was time consuming to locate his assets, when located they were registered properly. In the 25 years or so of being in the financial services industry I've seen a lot of estates but I've never seen anything quite like my uncle's.

I have no idea how many assets I've transferred for clients serving as trustees, but it was always just a piece of their estate. Presented with the challenge of an entire estate and one as complicated as my uncle's required a system. It was obvious that I needed a methodology to bring structure to the process.

The Notify-Respond-Verify system, or NRV, which you are about to explore, is the result of those many long hours of phone conversations, face-to-face meetings and written correspondence.

The Guide for the Successful Trustee – How it Works

The Guide for the Successful Trustee is designed to help you bring organization to the often overwhelming task of creating, managing and distributing an estate plan. The Guide has been developed by financial planners, attorneys and accountants with years of hands-on experience in dealing with estate planning needs of their clients. The Guide is not a legal document. It is, instead, a tool to get your estate in order, keep it in order and someday aid in the distribution of the estate to heirs. If The Guide accomplishes its' goals, a personalized system of asset monitoring and management that will help reduce taxes and improve income, is developed.

The Guide is divided into three sections. Each section represents a different phase of the estate planning cycle. Trustees don't necessarily need to start in Section One for The Guide to be beneficial. The Guide system of notification, response and verification has been designed with the typical estate in mind. However, since no two estates are identical, the services of an estate-planning attorney should be utilized. An attorney specializing in estate planning will know your options and be able to help you choose from the many financial planning options available. This guide will help in the implementation of your plan. The Guide is not a do it yourself manual.

The purpose of each section is to help you develop a methodology by which you can notify and track an asset that is being affected by a change in an estate plan. The forms needed to accomplish this task are provided in two formats, computer fillable (see Page 91 for details for the computer fillable version) or hand written. The goal is to notify an institution or individual of asset title changes and then follow through until the change in registration is completed.

The Guide does not produce legal documents; it makes the ones you do have work.

Each section of The Guide has forms unique to that phase. It is suggested that a 3-ring binder with labeled section tags be used to file all correspondence and statements. There are an infinite number of ways to organize your files as long as you are consistent with the notification system. Personally I separate my investment assets into qualified, non-qualified, life insurance and misc. sections then alphabetized under those four groups. No two estates are the same, so tailor your plan to fit your holdings. If the hand filled or manual method is chosen, fill out the asset identification new registration notification letter. Send the original form letter to the organization. Please print in black ink. Make a copy. At the same time fill out a log sheet for that asset. Place the log and the letter behind the appropriate tab and wait for the response. When the response is returned, comply with the request, indicate it on the log and place a copy in the appropriate binder section. Repeat the process until you have written documentation on all the changes requested. A follow-up letter should be forwarded to the asset if a reply is not received within two weeks of any communication.

It is recommended that any follow up with an asset include a copy of the reply correspondence that was returned by that asset initially. It never hurts to remind an organization of their initial request for additional documentation. There are many occasions when requirements seem to change from customer service agent to customer service agent at the same company.

Trustees need to stay current on the schedule of assets. Chasing assets that have been liquidated or that have changed locations can be confusing and very time consuming. When investments are exchanged or purchased the title needs to be changed promptly to the trust. A pour over will in a trust plan will "catch" assets so they can be distributed according to the trust terms. Assets distributed through the "pour over" will not avoid the cost and delay of probate.

A trustee who follows the Guide will develop a hard copy back up of all financial transactions. A one-location listing will allow trustees to access any information needed to manage or distribute trust assets for an estate. No matter how paperless our systems become, there will still be the need for original signatures.

Section 1 - Creation of Estate Plan

Place Family Photo

For the sake of this publication we will be referring to the creation of a trust-based estate plan as the development of an "estate plan". Because not all situations require a trust or trusts, it is very important to consult with a qualified estate planning attorney to review each family's needs. This guide may still be an excellent tool for the organization of assets, even if the situation does not require a trust. However, if a probate is required, please note that there are very specific procedures, forms and deadline requirements that vary from state to state and court to court, and a qualified probate attorney should be consulted.

It is critical to the success of any estate plan to get off to a good start. The better grasped this section is, the easier future sections will be. This guide does not generate legal documents. Rather, the guide helps establish a record keeping system of correspondence between an individual or family and the financial institutions and businesses with which they do transactions.

Typical assets that may need a change of registration when a trust is funded include, but are not limited to: stocks, mutual funds, bank accounts, real estate, bonds, re-investment accounts, money markets, etc. Assets that typically don't change title but may require a change of beneficiary include retirement plans, annuities and life insurance. These organizations may well have their own proprietary forms used to change beneficiaries. You may need to contact them for a change of beneficiary form.

Attorneys will not automatically transfer those assets which are changing title or beneficiary. However, if they do transfer assets, they may very well charge at their hourly rate. If you are apprehensive about the requirements of a particular asset, by all means spend the extra money to consult an attorney. Accountants, attorneys and financial planners agree that failure to fund or to properly fund a trust are the primary reasons trusts do not accomplish the goals of the grantee or grantors.

The time has been spent with the attorney formulating the plan. The check has been written to pay for it. Now comes the time to fund the trust. "Funding a trust" is estate-planning jargon for transferring assets to the trust. As soon as possible the trustee needs to re-register title on those assets affected by the creation of the trust.

It is very important that trustees understand the difference between the parties to all insurance contracts and retirement plan assets. The parties can be owner, beneficiary, insured, annuitant or insurer.

Owners are also known as grantors, trustors, settlors or participants. Trusts and other non-natural entities can be owners as well. "Incidents of Ownership" exist when the individual or entity has full or partial control of the contract. Incidents of Ownership are important when determining tax liability.

Beneficiaries are the parties designated to receive income, proceeds or tax savings created by the insurance policy or retirement plan.

The insured is the person or persons whose death triggers the payment of the death benefit to the beneficiary. The cost of the insurance is determined by his/her life expectancy.

The annuitant is similar to the insured in a life insurance contract. The life expectancy of the annuitant is used to set payment amounts on annuity contracts.

The insurer is the organization that will, for a premium payment, under-write protection as outlined in the contract.

The complexities of ownership make it imperative that all of the parties understand their roles and responsibilities in all transactions. Always consult with qualified legal and tax advisors before making any changes to estate planning documents or retirement funds.

The problems generally come up when working with the different treatment of Qualified and non-Qualified funds. Qualified, or retirement plan funds like IRAs, 401Ks and pension plans are treated differently from non-qualified funds in the tax code. Don't mix up the two types of funds. If you are not sure, ask the attorney. It can get very disorganized and expensive if the assets are not treated properly.

The process of transferring is really quite simple, but may be a little tedious.

- The first step is to notify the proper institutions of the changes that have been made.

- The second stage is to track the response from the institution and complete their requirements for transfer.

- The third step is to get verification from the institution contacted that your requested change has been made.

Get hard copy (written) documentation on all communication. You never know when you will need it. Not all transfer agents are created equal. Expect mistakes. The forms that appear in Appendix A, Section 1 have been developed to accomplish the transfers associated with the creation phase. Spend some time, get organized, and simplify your life, use The Guide.

When you are making a list of assets for your attorney, group your financial statements according to cash, qualified, non-qualified, and life insurance assets. (If an estate has additional trust assets, i.e. Charitable Remainder or Special Needs assets, make sure to keep them segregated from the other holdings.) Secure a three ring binder, punch holes in the statements and place them in reverse chronological order with the most recent statement on top. If the most recent statement includes all of the current years' transactions you may shred the old statements. If any transactions have occurred that aren't reflected on the statements, save your confirms as they may be needed for future tax reporting issues. Also, make sure to keep all fiscal year-end and 12/31 statements. You might want to include a copy of all 1099's in this section as well.

Next, following the statements, insert the written communications. A separate dated log should be established and maintained to help you remain organized for future reference.

Also of importance: in our income tax system, the *type* of asset is given precedence over investment *vehicle* when determining probate and tax treatment. For example, an IRA funded with mutual funds is an IRA first and a mutual fund second. In other words, you may hear an IRA referred to as the "type" or "flavor" of the money and the mutual fund is the "vehicle". Make sure to understand the terminology. An incorrect beneficiary, a mis-titled owner or a misfiled document can all confuse a trustee or a custodian and perhaps trigger a tax.

A properly created, funded and maintained estate plan will allow its creators to direct and control their assets well after they are gone. Taxes and probate can be reduced or eliminated, leaving more for friends and heirs, church and schools, pets, beneficiaries and favorite charities.

Section One dealt with getting organized and preparing for the eventualities in the next two phases: Transition and Settlement. The success or failure of an estate plan can rest upon the accuracy and organization of the paperwork. Assets must be properly titled in order that heirs and beneficiaries fully benefit from the time and money that goes into establishing the plan. Section One provides the communication system and documents needed to transfer assets to a living trust. If The Guide is maintained after the transfers are completed it can help with everything from taxes to transitions. It becomes an invaluable source of information for the Successful Trustee.

Section 1 - Notes:

Section 2 – Transition of Estate Plan

Place Family Photo

T he second phase of the estate planning cycle is the beginning of the actual asset transfer to beneficiaries. It is triggered by a significant event, the death or illness of a settlor, spouse or parent being the most common. Care issues can also trigger the need for implementation of the strategies outlined in the estate plan.

Since it is usually a negative event that triggers the transition phase, it is important that the appointed trustee be organized. There may be considerable stress when handling the other legal, personal and public pressures that can arise at a difficult time.

It is important that those involved in the management of the trust be notified as to their roles in the estate plan. Generally speaking, 'no surprises' is the rule of thumb here. It is best to answer any questions and settle any differences promptly without the pressures of a loved one's death or illness. Quite often someone named as a trustee will decline the position. Hopefully, the plan names a list of other potential successor/trustees. If not, the trustees could be in for a surprise at an inopportune time. Unless the trust states how a vacancy in the office of trustee may be filled, a petition must be brought before the Probate Court for the appointment of a successor trustee. Since avoiding the time and expense of probate proceedings was probably a major goal in creating the trust it would be unfortunate to require them after all.

Notification of beneficiaries is a different matter. Revealing who is getting what and when they are getting it is best left to the final or distribution phase.

An exception to this notification process could be gifts left to charity. Depending on the size and nature of the gift; it may be wise to notify the charity without delay. It may be possible to structure the gift so that it will generate an immediate tax benefit. At this point the use of advanced trust planning may come into play, and the services of an estate planning team can be invaluable.

The tax code allows for a number of different types of trusts, (e.g. Charitable Remainder, Charitable Lead, Irrevocable Life Insurance, etc.) that provide for planning strategies that could substantially benefit donor, beneficiary, charity and family.

It is important to keep up to date on any changes that may occur to beneficiaries, settlors and trustees. Death, divorce, disease and changes in dependents are some of the events that can change the people in a plan. As life changes, so must the details of a good estate plan.

Changed circumstances may require entirely new documents, complete with new tax identification numbers. Tax identification numbers or ("TIN"s) for individuals are their Social Security Numbers; for other entities, they are often referred to as EINs, short for "Employer Identification Numbers." even though the Trust or other entity may not "employ" anyone. You must be very careful to assign the correct TINs to the proper accounts. It is often a little confusing when the estate plan uses an A/B Trust strategy, common for a married couple; on the first death a Credit Shelter Trust (also known as a Bypass Trust) is created that must obtain a TIN, and a Survivor's Trust is also created that uses the surviving spouse's Social Security number until the survivor dies, at which time it also must have a new TIN. Special Needs Trusts, Charitable Remainder Trusts, Charitable Lead Trusts, Irrevocable Life Insurance Trusts, etc. will all need separate TINS and separate registrations. Depending on what additional documents are established, the settlor should use titles that are similar yet distinct.

The title should indicate the type of trust i.e. Survivors Trust, Credit Shelter Trust, Irrevocable Life Insurance Trust etc., the trustees, grantors and the date. If the plan being established has more than one trust of the same type i.e. Charitable Remainder Trust it is recommended not to repeat titles and number them sequentially. Why? Banks, investment companies, transfer agents and other financial institutions process thousands of requests each year. A one digit change can be too similar and not distinct enough for a busy transfer agent or bank teller to notice.

The second phase of an estate plan is more complicated than the first; however if trustees have kept The Guide up to date, it will be much easier to meet the trust requirements. Many years may pass between the first two phases, but if maintained, using The Guide will save friends and family countless hours of needless frustration.

Appendix A and B include examples of five letters that can be used to notify most of the individuals or companies that need to be informed on the death or disability of the first settlor. Two very important organizations, the Post Office and Social Security (1-800-772-1213) cannot be contacted by mail. Each has very specific requirements for transitioning an estate and should be contacted in person by the Trustee.

During the transition phase of the estate plan, the trust goes to work to accomplish the goals of the settlors. Assets are positioned to protect income for the surviving spouse and maximize values for the ultimate beneficiaries. In The Guide Section Two, five different groups are identified as people or organizations that will need to be contacted. Continue to keep The Guide up to date and Section Three, Distribution, will be a far less difficult task.

Section 2 - Notes:

Section 3 – Settlement of Estate Plan

Place Family Photo

When people think of being a trustee, Section Three of The Guide is more than likely the phase they are thinking about, probably because it can be the most difficult. If the estate has been properly maintained, as outlined in the previous two sections, the final settlement of accounts should proceed smoothly. "The distribution process or "settlement process" as it is also known, is the same as the creation and transition process: notify, respond and verify. The major differences between this phase and the previous two phases are volume and timing; there is a lot more to do and some filing dates that must be met.

Generally referred to as the "successor trustee", the trustee in the distribution phase will be dealing with a lot more than just assets. (Any trustee taking office after the initial trustee stops acting is a "successor trustee".) There may be utilities to notify, credit card accounts to close out, Social Security to deal with, property to manage, as well as taxes to be filed. The list of responsibilities can be a long one, depending upon the complexity of the estate to be settled. The successor trustee will also have to become familiar with filing dates for the different organizations and agencies. Becoming involved with the whys, what's, when's and wherefores of a settlor's life can be a trying experience. Accepting the task of closing out the financial and personal responsibilities of the Trustor can be a difficult one. There is a lot more to the role than simply passing out assets to heirs and beneficiaries.

What follows is an overview of actions that successor trustees need to take to address their responsibilities. The advisory team (accountant, attorney and financial planner) should be able to produce a more complete and time sensitive list.

However, before the estate can be settled, two important questions need to be addressed.

First, if the trustee feels as though the estate settlement process will require too much time or effort, now is a good time to resign. There is no legal requirement to accept the task. The job should only be accepted if the level of commitment is adequate. This Guide can be a real time-saver with the NRV system, but settling an estate still requires a certain level of dedication.

Second, the trustee's responsibility is to carry out the directions of the trust according to the estate documents and state probate and trust administration laws. The trustee needs to resist the temptation to administer the estate the way he/she thinks the settlor would have liked. Settling the estate in a way other than outlined in the trust documents can open the trustee up to civil and criminal action by the creditors and beneficiaries. Dealing with a disgruntled family member is often a trying experience. Be prepared.

Successor Trustee Checklist

- Locate Estate Documents. These include trusts, wills and financial powers. Note that financial powers of attorney terminate on the death of the Creator. These documents will give the trustee a road map to follow.

- Locate the original signed will. The will needs to be filed with the probate court. If the Trust was not properly funded, a probate may need to be opened. Being named Executor in a Will grants no powers until the appointment has been approved by the state Probate Court and Letters Testamentary have been issued.

- Contact advisors. Phone the attorney, accountant, financial planner, etc. of the deceased.

- Request the attorney or accountant to apply for a new Tax Identification Number. It will be needed to open up an account for payment of expenses and of settling the trust. (The estate plan may have included a joint account with the trustee for this purpose.)

- Locate recent income tax returns.

- Locate financial statements. Keep an eye out for assets that are not registered in the trust.
- Look for the following:
  Bank Accounts – Checking, Savings, CDs, Money Markets, Safe Deposit Box Receipts

  Credit Union Statements

  Trust Deeds

  Grant Deeds for Real Estate

  Credit Cards

  Brokerage Accounts and Confirmations

  Life Insurance and Annuity Statements

  Mutual Fund Statements

  Pension and Benefit Payment Receipts

- Order Death Certificates – The mortuary may be able to help. Estimate that one certificate per asset will be required. If a pension or annuity payment is involved, they too will require an original.
- Publish necessary announcements in newspaper. Mortuary may be able to help here also.

- Visit safe deposit boxes – When a box is first opened take along a witness to verify contents.

- Order appraisals for real estate and other tangible assets. Establish date of death values for taxes and probate fees. Alternate date rules could save the estate thousands. The attorney should know what is best. Note: if the assets were not in a trust, and are subject to probate, most assets will need to be appraised by an appraiser appointed by the Probate Court.

- Establish Notification System – Notify, Respond and Verify (NRV). Start NRV process with – Government agencies: a personal trip to the Post Office and Social Security. Military, teachers, police, fire departments etc. first. Government offices usually take the longest, so get them started quickly.

- Secure, protect and manage tangible assets. Make contact with tenants. Separate rents and expenses into pre and post date of death accounts.

- Catalog personal assets jewelry, art, antiques, collectibles, etc.

- Contact service groups like gardeners, house cleaners, care givers, utilities, etc. Keep separate records for before and after date of death.

- Establish any continuing trust shares. Commonly used to protect assets inherited by minor children. Special Needs Trust (SNTs) for mentally and physically challenged beneficiaries may also have been established by the decedent during life, but not funded until death through a share of the living trust.

- Pay the taxes. Final individual income tax returns, fiduciary income tax returns, and possibly an estate tax return will be completed based on some of the correspondence received. Keep the before and after date of death records separate.

Most of the individuals and companies that need to be contacted can be notified using one of five letters found in the Appendix. Make sure a matching correspondence is also placed in the log. The blank form letters are located in the Appendix immediately following Section Three . Two of the more important organizations, Social Security (1-800-772-1213) and the post office should be reached by phone (ok) or in person (better) to start the process as each has their own paperwork.

Section Three illustrates the need for a system to handle the sizeable amount of paperwork that can be generated when settling an estate. It also points out the importance of choosing a competent executor with the time and energy to stay on top of the task. Settling and distributing an estate is not a simple task. It is best to get organized early and keep it that way. That's one of the greatest gifts you can give.

Section 3 – Notes

GUIDE FOR THE SUCCESSFUL TRUSTEE
APPENDIX – HAND FILLED INSTRUCTIONS, LETTERS AND LOGS

Hand Filled Instructions, Letters and Logs

Place Family Photo

This section contains the nuts and bolts of the Guide for the trustee that prefers form letters and a more hands on approach to the Notify, Respond and Verify system. The section is divided into the three phases of an estate plan: Creation, Transition and Distribution.

Simply fill in the blanks using the definitions supplied and mail to the organization. Please print in black ink, it makes for better copies later on. When you mail the initial letter, make an entry in your log. You should hear back within two weeks; if not, re-mail a second request. If a third request is needed, try a form of delivery that requires a signature i.e. Fed-Ex, registered mail, etc.

What you will get back will be a request for additional information and documentation. Be alert to any special requests i.e. Notarized Signature, Signature Guarantee, etc.

Remember the difference between "change in beneficiary" and "change in registration". It makes a difference; make sure you get clear direction from your advisors.

If it is a beneficiary change that you need, request one from the organization in your initial letter. Request for a Change of Beneficiary Form appears at the end of Section One in this appendix.

Place the correspondence behind the log in the binder for that individual or organization and you're underway.

A couple of points to remember about the forms found in The Guide:

> There is no extra credit awarded for creative design. There are no prizes for originality of content. The best letters are the easiest for the processor to read and enter data from. They should be simple and to the point.

> Next, and this is important, make sure the original form letter is not filled in. Make your blank copies first, you will need them later. A slipcover, that the letter can be placed into for protection can work. Laminating the original might be a good option if there are a large number of contacts or asset listings involved.

Data Collection and transfer forms for real estate transactions are purposely omitted from The Guide because of the complexity involved. Title registration varies from state to state. Trustees will need to contact local real estate professionals or an attorney for the appropriate procedures.

When filling out letters to the individuals and institutions that must be notified when there are changes in an estate plan, the executor or trustee must understand the differences between "owner" and "trustee", "beneficiary" and "insured" and "grantor". Not knowing the nuances of estate planning can create confusion, probate and taxes. The best defense against possible problems is a good team of advisors. The three critical professions to a successful estate plan are attorney, accountant and financial advisor. The attorney is responsible for knowing how to establish a plan, the accountant knows how much it costs (or saves) and the financial advisor gets it done.

The Guide is a tool designed to help organize, maintain and ultimately settle an estate. It is not a guarantee that the plan designed is the best possible plan available. As with most legal documents, language is everything. The following information examines the terminology used in the process.

Qualified funds (retirement plans) provide some of the most confusing language. Qualified funds are assets that receive special tax treatment by law. They are participant driven (owner), held by a custodian and maintained by an administrator. The funds are invested by a fund manager for the benefit of (FBO) the owner. Generally, upon the death of the owner, the remaining funds are transferred to the surviving spouse (spousal beneficiary). Non-spousal beneficiaries can be, but are not limited to: children, grand-children, charities, trusts, etc. Please consult with qualified tax and legal advisors for information as to how the laws affect you and your family.

Trusts have three interested parties.

1.   Settlors, Trustmakers, Creators, Grantors and Trustors, are titles used by the individuals that create and fund the trust. They determine all the terms of the trust; including who will be named successor trustees and the timing and the amount of distribution to the beneficiaries. They are responsible for funding their assets into the trust, through re-titling and beneficiary designation.

Only the settlors can change the terms of their trust, and only if or while the trust is revocable.

The settlors may be an individual (natural) or a business (non-natural). Most of the financial benefits, tax savings, income and principal increases are generated to the settlors.

2.   The Trustee, (Director or Manager) is responsible for the Management of the trust in accordance with the terms of the trust and in compliance with state and federal laws. Trustees may be individuals, trust companies, banks etc. Trustees may, in some cases, also be settlors. In some trusts trustees must be completely independent and cannot be beneficiaries.

In most cases, settlors are also the trustees of their family trusts; however in some specialized types of trusts, the settlors may not receive all the benefits and protections available if they are also the trustees.

In still other arrangements successor trustees are the same persons as the ultimate beneficiaries, but again, in some types of trusts this is not permissible, and in others it may not be advisable.

3.   The third interested party in a trust is the beneficiary. The beneficiary can receive a current income benefit, a future lump sum or a tax deduction. Beneficiaries can also be another trust or trusts to benefit a special needs situation. Beneficiaries may include a charity for current income, Charitable Lead Trust or, a future lump sum, Charitable Remainder Trust.

Section 1 - Data Collection - Trust Definitions and Information Instructions

Place Family Photo

Trustor – Settlor, Creator, Grantor of trust. Name should appear on first page of trust document. Enter exactly as the entry appears on new trust, one name per line.

Title of Trust – Full name of trust. Name should appear on first page of trust document. Fill in form with full name of trust including Trustor(s), Trustee(s) and Date.

SSN/TIN/EIN – Tax identification number of new trust. The tax ID that will be used on this asset for reporting of earnings on tax filings. If there is a previous number, enter on the Current SSN/TIN/EIN line.

Trustee - Person or firm that will manage or co-manage trust.

Date New Trust Created - Stated on signature and/or title page of document. Signature page generally appears on the last page of new trust document.

Contact/Trustee Information – Name(s) of individual(s) to be used for correspondence regarding matters of the trust. Please fill in completely. If relevant use Trustor or Trustee information.

Fill in the information requested to begin the transfer of your assets to a new trust.

Trust Information:

Settlor _____

Settlor_____

Title of New Trust_____

_____

Date New Trust Created _____

New SSN/TIN _____Current SSN/TIN_____

Trustee _____

Trustee _____

Contact Information:

Name _____

Street _____

Suite/Appt _____

City _____State_____ Zip _____

Section 1 - Data Collection – Asset/Contact Listing

Financial/Contact Organization – Name of individual or company i.e., (Acme Bank, ABC Brokers, and XYZ Life) that issued or holds the asset being transferred to the trust. Not for use as change in beneficiary form or qualified asset transfer request. The organization will probably require that you use their forms.

Asset/Contact Name – Product Marketing Name or Type of Account: Wells Fargo 9 Month CD, Fidelity Magellan, Scottrade Trading etc.

Asset/Contact Account Number – Identifying number issued with asset that distinguishes it from other assets issued by individual or company. Each account number should be listed on a separate form. This extra paperwork now will save you time and confusion later as the process (and your financial life) continues.

Account/Contact Address – Current location to mail all correspondence and forms to in order to complete the transfer of the existing asset to new trust. Often referred to as transfer address or transfer agent.

Unfortunately due to the processing differences from locality to locality real estate cannot be transferred with the forms provided. Please check with your attorney or appropriate government agency for complete instructions on transfer of real estate.

Asset/Contact Listing

Financial/Contact Organization_____

Check box that applies on the previous listing, check only one box.

O Asset   O Payor   O Creditor   O Service Provider   O Beneficiary

Asset Contact Name _____

Street _____

City _____

State _____ Zip _____

Account Number _____

Asset Description_____

Last 4 Digits of Tax Identification Number _____

Notes _____

_____

_____

_____

_____

Correspondence Tracking Log

Financial Institution
Check box that applies on the previous listing, check only one box.

O Asset   O Payor   O Creditor   O Service Provider   O Beneficiary

Asset/Contact/Number_____

Asset/Account/Number_____

Street_____

City_____ State_____ Zip_____

Notes_____

_____

_____

_____

Financial Organization Notification

Today's Date_____

Financial Organization _____

Asset Name_____

Street_____

City_____ State _____Zip_____

Asset Account Number_____

Please use this letter as your notification of the creation of a new trust for the assets currently held by your organization. The new registration is as follows:

Settlor _____

Settlor _____

Title of Trust _____

Date Trust Created_____

New SSN/TIN/EIN _____ Current SSN/TIN/EIN _____

Trustee _____

Trustee _____

Should any additional documentation be necessary please contact:

Name_____

Address_____

City _____State _____ Zip _____

Sincerely,

_____

Directory Listing for Financial Institutions

Financial Organization_____

Asset Name_____

Street_____

City_____ State _____Zip_____

Asset Account Number_____

Financial Organization _____

Asset Name_____

Street_____

City_____ State _____Zip_____

Asset Account Number_____

Financial Organization _____

Asset Name_____

Street_____

City_____ State _____Zip_____

Asset Account Number_____

Financial Organization _____

Asset Name_____

Street_____

City_____ State _____Zip_____

Asset Account Number_____

Change of Beneficiary Form Request (Retirement Plan)

Date _____

Account Owner _____

Account Number _____

Custodian _____

Address _____

City _____ State _____ Zip _____

Spouse _____

Current
Beneficiaries _____

Mail Form to Name _____

Address _____

City _____ State _____ Zip _____

Or E-Mail Form to _____

Please forward the forms and instructions necessary to change the beneficiary designation(s) on the referenced policy.

Owner Signature   Spouses Signature

_____

Change of Beneficiary Form Request

(Life Insurance Policy)

Date _____

Policy Owner _____

Policy Number_____

Policy Issuer _____

Address_____

City_____ State _____ Zip_____

Current Beneficiaries_____

Mail Form to Name_____

Address_____

City _____State _____ Zip _____

Or E-Mail Form to _____

Please forward the forms and instructions necessary to change the beneficiary designation(s) on the referenced policy.

Owner Signature   Spouses Signature

Change of Beneficiary Form Request

(Non-Life Insurance Policy)

Date _____

Policy Owner _____

Policy Number_____

Policy Issuer _____

Address_____

City_____ State _____ Zip_____

Current Beneficiaries_____

Mail Form to Name_____

Address_____

City _____State _____ Zip _____

Or E-Mail Form to _____

Please forward the forms and instructions necessary to change the beneficiary designation(s) on the referenced policy.

Owner Signature   Spouses Signature

_____

Section 1 – Notes

Section 2 - Data Collection - Trust Definitions and Information Instructions

Place Family Photo

The option introduces a very powerful feature for developing a record of the individuals and companies that you associate with. It can save trustees countless hours of research time. Creating and maintaining a directory of contacts will simplify the process that trustees face when transitioning and settling an estate. While it can be helpful (recommended) to divide contacts into the five categories listed in Section One; Letters of Notification do not need to be sent to the four non-financial contact categories until phase Two. Generally speaking the non-financial contacts aren't affected by the establishment of a trust so there's no need to be informed.

Asset – Letter -1.1 Banks, Credit Unions, Stocks, Bonds, Mutual Funds, Brokerage Houses, Investment Firms, Insurance Companies, Dividend Re-investment Plans, etc.

Payor – Letters 2.2 and 3.2 - Payors, annuity companies, pension plans, and welfare departments, veteran's agencies

Creditors – Letters 2.3 and 3.3 - Creditors, personal loans, installment sales, credit cards

Personal service – Letters 2.4 and 3.4 - Service contracts, utility companies, subscriptions

Beneficiaries – Letters 2.5 and 3.5 – Beneficiaries, charities, heirs, beneficial trusts

Data Collection – Trust Information

New Title of Trust – Full name of trust. Name should appear on first or title page of trust. Fill in form exactly as it appears on trust.

SSN/TIN/EIN – Tax identification number of new trust. Tax ID that will be used on this asset for reporting of earnings on tax filings.

Executor/Trustee - Person or firm that will manage final trust distribution.

Date New Trust Created – As stated on signature page of Trust. Signature page generally appears on the last page of new trust.

Contact Information – Name(s) of individual(s) to be used for correspondence regarding matters of trust. Please fill in completely. Use Trustor or Trustee information if relevant.

Deceased Trustor – Name of individual that through death, disability or resignation is no longer able to manage trust assets.

Date of Death of Trustor – Date of death as indicated on death certificate or court documents.

Original Title of Trust – Exact title of original trust.

Current SSN/TIN/EIN – Current number being used for the tax reporting on trust earnings.

Original Trustee – Trustee of original trust documents.

Date of Original Trust – Date on original trust document title page.

Trust Information

New Title of Trust _____

_____

New SSN/TIN _____ Current SSN/TIN_____

New Trustee _____

New Trustee _____

Date new trust created _____

Contact Information:

Name _____

Street _____

City _____ State _____ Zip _____

Deceased Settlor _____

Surviving Settlor _____

Date of Death _____

Original Title of Trust _____

Original Trustee _____

Original Trustee _____

Date original trust created _____

Section 2 - Data Collection – Asset/Contact Listing

Financial/Contact Organization – Name of individual or company i.e., (Acme Bank, ABC Brokers, XYZ Life) that issued or holds the asset being transferred to the trust. Not for use as change in beneficiary form or qualified asset transfer request. The organization will probably require that you use their forms.

Asset/Contact Name – Product Marketing Name or Type of Account: Wells Fargo 9 month CD, Fidelity Magellan, Scottrade Trading, etc.

Asset/Contact Account Number – Identifying number issued with asset that distinguishes it from other assets issued by individual or company. Each account number should be listed on a separate form. This extra paperwork now will save you time and confusion later as the process (and your financial life) continues.

Account/Contact Address – Current location to mail all correspondence and forms to in order to begin the transfer of the existing asset to new trust. Often referred to as transfer address or transfer agent.

Unfortunately due to the processing differences from locality to locality real estate cannot be transferred with the forms provided. Please check with your attorney or appropriate government agency for complete instructions on transfer of real estate.

Asset/Contact Listing

Financial Organization _____

Financial Contact _____

Check box that applies on the previous listing, check only one box.

O Asset   O Payor   O Creditor   O Service Provider   O Beneficiary

Asset/Contact Name_____

Street _____

City _____

State _____ Zip _____

Last 4 Digits of Tax Identification Number _____

Section 2 – Notes:

Section 2 – Letters

Letter 2.1 - To be used for – Banks, Credit Unions, Stocks, Bonds, Mutual Funds, Brokerage Houses, Investment Firms, Insurance Companies, Dividend Re-investment Plans, etc.

Letter 2.2 -To be used for – annuity payments, pension payors, welfare departments, veteran agencies, etc.

Letter 2.3 - To be used for – creditors, personal loans, credit cards, installment payment plans, etc.

Letter 2.4 - To be used for - service providers, utilities, personal service contracts, subscriptions, contract personal service providers, etc.

Letter 2.5 - To be used for notification of beneficiaries and charities.

2.1 - Authorization to Financial Institution

Correspondence Tracking Log

Check box that applies to this log, check only one box.
O Asset   O Payor   O Creditor   O Service Provider   O Beneficiary

Contact/Asset name_____

Account number_____

Street_____

City_____ State_____ Zip_____

Notes_____

_____

_____

_____

_____

_____

_____

_____

_____

_____

Date transfer completed_____

Authorization to Financial Institution

Date_____

Financial Institution_____

Asset Name_____

Street_____

City_____

State_____ Zip_____

Asset Account Number_____

New SSN/TIN _____ Current SSN/TIN_____

Please use this letter of authorization and enclosed death certificate to transfer all accounts held by your institution to the new registration detailed below.

New Title of Trust_____

New Settlor _____

New Settlor _____

Date Trust Created_____

Should any additional documentation be necessary to complete this transaction please contact:

Name_____

Street_____

City_____

State_____Zip_____

Executor/Trustee

Signature

2.2 – Letter to Institutions to Discontinue or Modify Benefits

Correspondence Tracking Log

Check box that applies to this log, check only one box.
O Asset   O Payor   O Creditor   O Service Provider   O Beneficiary

Contact/Asset name_____

Account number_____

Street_____

City_____State_____Zip_____

Notes_____

_____

_____

_____

_____

_____

_____

_____

_____

_____

Date transfer completed_____

_____

Letter to Institutions to Discontinue or Modify Benefits

Date_____

Institution_____

Street_____

City_____

State _____Zip_____

Asset Account Number_____

Please accept the enclosed death certificate and this letter to inform you of the death of:
Name Deceased _____Date of Death_____

Please discontinue or alter benefits per contract. Please note a change in SSN/TIN

New SSN/TIN_____ Current SSN/TIN_____

If benefits include spousal or other annuity payments, please commence those payments.

If there are forms needed for any lump sum distributions please forward those requests to:

Name_____

Street_____

City_____

State _____Zip_____

Executor/Trustee

Signature

2.3 – Notification to Creditors

Correspondence Tracking Log

Check box that applies to this log, check only one box.
O Asset   O Payor   O Creditor   O Service Provider   O Beneficiary

Contact/Asset name_____

Account number_____

Street_____

City_____ State_____ Zip_____

Notes_____

_____

_____

_____

_____

_____

_____

_____

_____

_____

_____

Date transfer completed_____

_____

Notification to Creditors

Date_____

Creditor _____

Business Name_____

Street_____

City_____

State_____ Zip _____

Account Number_____

Please accept the enclosed death certificate and this letter to inform you of the death of:

Deceased Name _____Date_____

According to your policy :(Choose One)

O Please close this account.
O Please close this account and open a new account in the name of the surviving spouse.
O Please maintain this account and remove the name of the deceased.

Please send any forms, applications or statements to the following address.

Name_____

Street_____

City_____

State_____Zip_____

Sincerely,

Executor/Trustee

Signature

2.4 – Notification to Service Providers

Correspondence Tracking Log

Check box that applies to this log, check only one box.
O Asset   O Payor   O Creditor   O Service Provider O Beneficiary

Contact/Asset Name_____

Account Number _____

Street_____

City_____

State _____ Zip_____

Notes_____

_____

_____

_____

_____

_____

_____

_____

_____

_____

Notification to Service Providers

Date_____

Individual or Business_____

Department or Contact_____

Street _____

City _____

State_____ Zip _____

Account Number_____ _____

Please accept the enclosed death certificate and this letter to inform you of the death of:

Deceased Name_____ Date _____
O Discontinue your service to the deceased's address and forward a closing statement to the address below.
O Continue your existing service uninterrupted and change the billing address to the address below.
O Please forward any documentation needed for a change of customer at the same service address.

Please send any forms, applications or statements to the following address.

Name_____

Street_____

City_____

State_____Zip_____

Executor/Trustee

Signature

_____

2.5 – Notification of Beneficiaries

Correspondence Tracking Log

Check box that applies to this log, check only one box.
O Asset O Payor O Creditor O Service Provider   O Beneficiary

Contact/Asset Name _____

Account Number _____

Street_____

City_____ State_____ Zip_____

Notes _____

_____

_____

_____

_____

_____

_____

_____

Date transfer completed _____

_____

Notification of Beneficiaries

Date_____

Individual or Charity_____

Contact _____

Street _____

City_____

State_____ Zip_____

As Executor/Trustee I am required to notify you of the death of

_____ on _____

Please direct all requests for information to the address below.

Contact Information

Name _____

Street_____

City _____

State _____Zip_____

Sincerely,

Executor/Trustee

2.6 - Directory Listing for Organizations/Contacts

Check box that applies to this list, check only one box.
O Asset   O Payor   O Creditor   O Service Provider   O Beneficiary

Organization_____

Reference/Asset Name_____

Street_____

City_____ State _____ Zip _____

Account Number_____

Organization _____

Reference/Asset Name _____

Street_____

City_____ State _____ Zip_____

Account Number_____

Organization _____

Reference/Asset Name_____

Street_____

City _____ State _____ Zip_____

Account Number_____

Organization _____

Reference/Asset Name_____

Street_____

City_____ State _____ Zip _____

Account Number_____

Section 2 – Notes:

Section 3 - Data Collection – Trust Information

Place Family Photo

New Title of Trust – Full name of trust. Name should appear on cover page of trust. Fill in form exactly as it appears on trust.

SSN/TIN/EIN – Tax identification # of new trust. Tax ID that will be used on this asset for reporting of earnings on tax filings.

Executor/Trustee - Person or firm that will manage final trust distribution.

Date New Trust Created - Stated on signature page of document. Signature page generally appears on the last page of new trust document.

Contact Information – Name(s) of individual(s) to be used for correspondence regarding matters trust. Please fill in completely. Use Trustor or Trustee information if relevant.

Deceased Settlor – Name of individual that through death, disability or resignation is no longer able to manage trust assets.

Date of Death of Settlor – Date of death as indicated on death certificate or court documents.

Original Title of Trust – Exact title of original trust.

Current SSN/TIN/EIN – Current number being used for the tax reporting on trust earnings.

Original Trustee – Trustee of original trust documents.

Date Original Trust Created – Date on original trust document title page.

Trust Data Collection Form

New Title of Trust _____

New Trustee_____

New Trustee _____

Asset Account Number_____

Date of New Trust _____

Contact Information

Name_____

Street_____

City_____

State_____ Zip_____

Deceased Settlor_____

Date of Death_____

Original Title _____

Original Trustee _____

Original Trustee_____

Date original trust created _____

Section 3 - Data Collection – Asset/Contact Listing

Financial/Contact Organization – Name of individual or company i.e., (Acme Bank, ABC Brokers, XYZ Life) that issued or holds the asset being transferred to the trust. Not for use as change in beneficiary form or qualified asset transfer request. The organization will probably require that you use their forms.

Asset/Contact Name – Product Marketing Name or Type of Account: Wells Fargo 9 month CD, Fidelity Magellan, Scottrade Trading, etc.

Asset/Contact Account Number – Identifying number issued with asset that distinguishes it from other assets issued by individual or company. Each account number should be listed on a separate form. This extra paperwork now will save you time and confusion later as the process (and your financial life) continues.

Account/Contact Address – Current location to mail all correspondence and forms to in order to complete the transfer of the existing asset to new trust. Often referred to as transfer address or transfer agent.

Unfortunately due to the processing differences from locality to locality real estate cannot be transferred with the forms provided. Please check with your attorney or appropriate government agency for complete instructions on transfer of real estate.

Asset/Contact Listing Form

Check box that applies on the previous listing, check only
one box. Section 1 Assets only.

O Asset   O Payor   O Creditor   O Service Provider   O Beneficiary

Financial/Contact
Organization_____

Asset/Contact Name _____

Street _____

City_____

State _____ Zip _____

Account Number

_____

Last 4 Digits of Tax Identification Number (TIN)

_____

Notes:

Section 3 – Letters

Letter 3.1 - To be used for – Banks, Credit Unions, Stocks, Bonds, Mutual Funds, Brokerage Houses, Investment Firms, Insurance Companies, Dividend Re-investment Plans, etc.

Letter 3.2 -To be used for – annuity payments, pension payors, welfare departments, veteran agencies, etc.

Letter 3.3 - To be used for – creditors, personal loans, credit cards, installment payment plans, etc.

Letter 3.4 - To be used for - service providers, utilities, personal service contracts, subscriptions, contract personal service providers, etc.

Letter 3.5 - To be used for notification of beneficiaries and charities.

3.1 – Letter to Financial Organizations

Correspondence Tracking Log

Check box that applies to this log, check only one box.
O Asset   O Payor   O Creditor O Service provider O Beneficiary

Contact/Asset name_____

Account Number _____

Street_____

City_____ State _____ Zip_____

Notes_____

_____

_____

_____

_____

_____

_____

_____

_____

_____

Date transfer completed_____

Letter to Financial Organizations

Date_____

Financial Organization _____

Asset Name_____

Street_____

City_____

State_____ Zip _____

Please use this letter and copy of death certificate to notify you of the death of:

Deceased: _____ Date _____

Also enclosed is a copy of the title page and appointment page naming the trustee. Please forward to the address below any instructions and documentation that will be needed for the settlement of this estate.

Sincerely,

Executor/Trustee

Name_____

Street_____

City_____

State_____ Zip_____

3.2 – Letter to Institutions to Discontinue or Modify Benefits

Correspondence Tracking Log

Check box that applies to this log, check only one box.
O Asset   O Payor   O Creditor   O Service Provider   O Beneficiary

Contact/Asset name_____

Account Number _____

Street_____

City_____ State_____ Zip_____

Notes_____

_____

_____

_____

_____

_____

_____

_____

_____

_____

Date transfer completed_____

Letter to Institutions to Discontinue or Modify Benefits

Date_____

Institution_____

Street _____

City_____

State_____ Zip_____

Account Number _____

Please accept the enclosed death certificate and this letter to inform you of the death of:

Deceased Name_____ Date _____

Please discontinue or alter benefits per contract.

If benefits include continued payments or a lump sum distribution please forward any claims paperwork to:

Name_____

Street_____

City_____

State_____ Zip_____

Sincerely,

Executor/Trustee

3.3 – Notification to Creditors

Correspondence Tracking Log

Check box that applies to this log, check only one box.
O Asset   O Payor   O Creditor   O Service Provider   O Beneficiary

Contact/Asset name_____

Account Number _____

Street_____

City_____ State _____ Zip_____

Notes_____

_____

_____

_____

_____

_____

_____

_____

_____

_____

Date transfer completed_____

Notification to Creditors

Date_____

Creditor _____

Business Name_____

Street_____

City_____

State_____ zip _____

Account Number_____

Please accept the enclosed death certificate and this letter to inform you of the death of:

Deceased Name_____ Date _____

According to your policy: (Choose One)

O Please close this account.
O Please close this account and open a new account in the name of the surviving spouse.
O Please maintain this account and remove the name of the deceased.

Please send any forms, applications or statements to the following address.

Name_____

Street_____

City_____

State _____ Zip _____

Sincerely
Executor

3.4 - Notification to Service Providers

Correspondence Tracking Log

Check box that applies to this log, check only one box.
O Asset   O Payor   O Creditor   O Service Provider   O Beneficiary

Contact/Asset name_____

Account Number _____

Street_____

City_____ State _____ Zip_____

Notes_____

_____

_____

_____

_____

_____

_____

_____

_____

Date transfer completed_____

Notification to Service Providers

Date_____

Individual or Business_____

Department or Contact_____

Street _____

City _____

State_____ Zip_____

Account Number_____

Please accept this letter and enclosed copy of death certificate as notification of the death

Of _____ on _____

Choose one:

O Discontinue your service to the deceased's address and forward a closing statement to the address below.

O Continue your existing service uninterrupted and change the billing address to the address below.

O Please forward any documentation needed for a change of customer at the same service address.

Sincerely,

Executor/Trustee

Name _____

Street_____

City_____ State _____ Zip _____

3.5– Notification of Beneficiaries

Correspondence Tracking Log

Check box that applies to this log, check only one box.
O Asset   O Payor   O Creditor   O Service Provider   O Beneficiary

Contact/Asset name_____

Account Number _____

Street_____

City_____ State _____ Zip _____

Notes_____

_____

_____

_____

_____

_____

_____

_____

_____

_____

Date transfer completed_____

_____

Notification of Beneficiaries

Date_____

Individual or Charity_____

Contact _____

Street _____

City_____ State _____ Zip _____

As Executor/Trustee I am required to notify you of the death of

_____ on _____.

Please direct all requests for information to the address below.

Contact Information

Name _____

Street_____

City _____

State_____ Zip _____

Sincerely,

Executor/Trustee

3.6 - Directory Listing for Organizations/Contacts

Check box that applies to this list, check only one box.
O Asset   O Payor   O Creditor   O Service Provider   O Beneficiary

Organization _____

Reference Asset Name _____

Street _____

City _____ State _____ Zip _____

Account Number _____

Organization _____

Reference Asset Name _____

Street _____

City _____ State _____ Zip _____

Account Number _____

Organization _____

Reference Asset Name _____

Street _____

City _____ State _____ Zip _____

Account Number _____

Organization _____

Reference Asset Name _____

Street _____

City _____ State _____ Zip _____

Account Number _____

Section 3 – Notes:

Section 3 – Beneficiary Page

This page is a quick reference index of the beneficiaries named on qualified money accounts, annuity and life insurance contracts and other funds that will pass directly to heirs at death.

Name _____ Name _____

Social Security # _____ Social Security # _____

Date of Birth _____ Date of Birth _____

Relationship _____ Relationship _____

Account _____ Account _____

Name _____ Name _____

Social Security # _____ Social Security # _____

Date of Birth _____ Date of Birth _____

Relationship _____ Relationship _____

Account _____ Account _____

Name _____ Name _____

Social Security # _____ Social Security # _____

Date of Birth _____ Date of Birth _____

Relationship _____ Relationship _____

Account _____ Account _____

Name _____ Name _____

Social Security # _____ Social Security # _____

Date of Birth _____ Date of Birth _____

Relationship _____ Relationship _____

Account _____ Account _____

Name _____ Name _____

Social Security # _____ Social Security # _____

Date of Birth _____ Date of Birth _____

Relationship _____ Relationship _____

Account _____ Account _____

The accounts have been closed, the taxes are current and the debts are all paid. The job is a wrap all done, go ahead and pay the heirs.

Getting Started With The Guide for the Successful Trustee

Now there remains only one question to be answered?

Manual or automated, hand-written or digital.

Which system will you use to access the benefits of the guide?

If you choose the manual method then you should have everything you need to get started. We suggest that you use a three ring binder for storage of all communications.

If you choose the automated version you will need to contact our client services area which can be found on our website (www.SharPointPub.com). Simply contact the address listed there and you will be instructed on how to receive your automated appendix.

In Conclusion

Please keep this guide available for future reference. Please use the contact information provided with this Appendix should you have questions and comments.

Glossary

401Ks - A defined contribution plan offered to employees by a corporation, which allows the employee to set aside tax-deferred income for retirement purposes.

403(b)s - Employer sponsored retirement savings plan for employees of charities, hospitals, colleges and other not for profit organizations.

A/B Trust - A type of trust strategy used by married couples to minimize estate taxes and increase control of assets at the first death. It involves dividing the estate into two trusts on the first death. The A Trust can be referred to as the Survivor's trust and the B Trust as the decedent's or bypass or shelter trust.

CDs - Certificates of Deposit. A time deposit purchased from banks that are insured up to a maximum amount established by the FDIC. All earnings are taxable.

Charitable Lead Trust – Charitable estate planning strategy that provides income to a qualifying charity for a term of years. When the term ends the remainder ordinarily goes back to the Settlor or the Settlor's beneficiaries.

Charitable Remainder Trust - A trust used primarily for gifts to charity. This type of trust allows the donor to retain income for the life of the donor(s) or a designated time period.

Credit Shelter Trust- Part of A/B Trust strategy that allows for the maximum usage of the first deceased spouse's exemption from estate taxes. This trust is also referred to as the B trust.

EIN - Internal Revenue Service terminology for tax identification in lieu of a social security number. Employee Identification Number.

Fixed Annuities - A contract with an insurance company that provides for a fixed interest rate over a fixed period of time. This product is not FDIC insured.

Grantors - Individuals or married couples that establish and fund trusts. May also be referred to as Trustor(s) or Settlor(s).

Income Annuities - A contract between parties where a cash deposit is exchanged for future income stream. Can also be referred to as an immediate annuity**.**

IRAs - Individual Retirement Accounts. Tax deferred saving accounts where funds are anticipated to be used for retirement. There are two basic types of IRA's, Traditional and Roth. A Traditional IRA's contributions are tax deductible and withdrawals are taxable. Contributions to a Roth IRA are not tax deductible. However, earnings and withdrawals are tax free.

Irrevocable Life Insurance Trust - A Permanent trust used to hold life insurance policies outside of taxable estate. Eliminates taxation on life insurance proceeds.

IRS - Internal Revenue Service

Letters Testamentary - Probate court document establishing representative power to conduct business on behalf of estate.

Living Trust - Revocable estate planning strategy used to create smooth transfer of assets from one generation to the next. This trust can be used to reduce taxes, avoid probate and extend control of assets after death. Like a will, a living trust defines who is entitled to which assets at death of Grantor/Trustor/Settlor.

Money Markets - Securities composed of short term debt instruments. Maturities may be as short as one day. Investments include corporate and government securities.

Non-Qualified - Investment assets that do not meet the IRS (or ERISA) requirements for favorable tax treatment.

Probate - A court supervised process by which the decedent's wishes are validated, or establishes distribution of assets if no will has been created.

Qualified - Retirement plan assets that receive special tax treatment as defined in the tax code i.e. IRAs, 401ks, 403bs, etc.

REITs - Real Estate Investment Trusts. A type of security that is composed of real estate based securities. Can be actual real estate, securities of real estate companies or mortgages, professionally managed pool of investor funds, etc.

Special Needs Trust - A trust created for the special needs of beneficiaries that are challenged mentally or physically. It allows the trustee to utilize property for the benefit of the designated party.

Survivors Trust - Created at first death of a married couple. Surviving spouse controls A trust and also is entitled to income from B trust.

Testamentary Trusts - Trusts that are created by the instructions of a will upon death.

TIN - Tax Identification Number used by IRS in lieu of Social Security Number.

Trustee(s) - The person(s) or company designated to manage the trust for the benefit of the beneficiaries. Also known as trust managers.

Trustor(s) - Person(s) that establish and fund the trust by transferring assets to the trust. Also known as grantor(s) or settlor(s).

Variable Annuity - Investment that has a rate of return that is not fixed but is affected by market fluctuations and the types of assets held in sub-accounts.